COLDPLAY · PARACHUTES

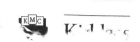

D1493609

250 591 812

Wise Publications
London / New York / Sydney / Paris / Copenhagen / Madrid / Tokyo

Exclusive distributors:
Music Sales Limited
8/9 Frith Street, London W1D 3JB, England.

Music Sales Pty Limited
120 Rothschild Avenue, Rosebery, NSW 2018, Australia.

Order No.AM970893
ISBN 0-7119-8924-9
This book © Copyright 2001 by Wise Publications.

Music arranged by Derek Jones.
Music engraved by Paul Ewers Music Design.

Printed in the United Kingdom by
Caligraving Limited, Thetford, Norfolk.

Your Guarantee of Quality:
As publishers, we strive to produce every book to the highest commercial standards.
The music has been freshly engraved and, whilst endeavouring
to retain the original running order of the recorded album, the book has been carefully
designed to minimise awkward page turns and to make playing from it a real pleasure.
Particular care has been given to specifying acid-free, neutral-sized
paper made from pulps which have not been elemental chlorine bleached.
This pulp is from farmed sustainable forests and
was produced with special regard for the environment.
Throughout, the printing and binding have been planned to ensure a sturdy,
attractive publication which should give years of enjoyment.
If your copy fails to meet our high standards, please inform us and we will gladly replace it.

Music Sales' complete catalogue describes thousands of titles and
is available in full colour sections by subject, direct from Music Sales Limited.
Please state your areas of interest and send a cheque/postal order for £1.50 for postage to:
Music Sales Limited, Newmarket Road, Bury St. Edmunds, Suffolk IP33 3YB.

www.musicsales.com

DON'T PANIC

Words & Music by Guy Berryman, Jon Buckland, Will Champion & Chris Martin

1, 2. Bones, sink - ing like stones, all ___ that we've fought ___ for. ___
(Verse 3 Instrumental)

Homes, pla - ces we've grown, all ___ of us are

4

Oh, all— that I know, there's no-thing here to run from,— cos

yeah, ev-'ry-bo-dy here's got some-bo-dy to lean on.—

SHIVER

Words & Music by Guy Berryman, Jon Buckland, Will Champion & Chris Martin

look in your di-rec-tion but you pay me no at-ten-tion do you?
(Verse 2 see block lyric)

And I

know you don't lis-ten to me cos you say you see straight through me don't

you? But on and on

Verse 2:
So you know how much I need you
But you never even see me do you?
And is this my final chance of getting you?

But on and on, from the moment I wake *etc.*

SPIES

Words & Music by Guy Berryman, Jon Buckland, Will Champion & Chris Martin

And— if we don't hide— here they're gon-na find us.

Spies came out of the wa - ter and you're feel- ing so good 'cause you know that those spies hide out in e-ve-ry cor - ner and they can't touch

Verse 2:
I awake to see that no-one is free
We're all fugitives
Look at the way we live
Down here I cannot sleep from fear, no
I said, "Which way do I turn?"
Oh, I forget ev'rything I learn.

And the spies came out of the water *etc.*

SPARKS

Words & Music by Guy Berryman, Jon Buckland, Will Champion & Chris Martin

Guitar: Tune 1st string to D, capo 6th fret

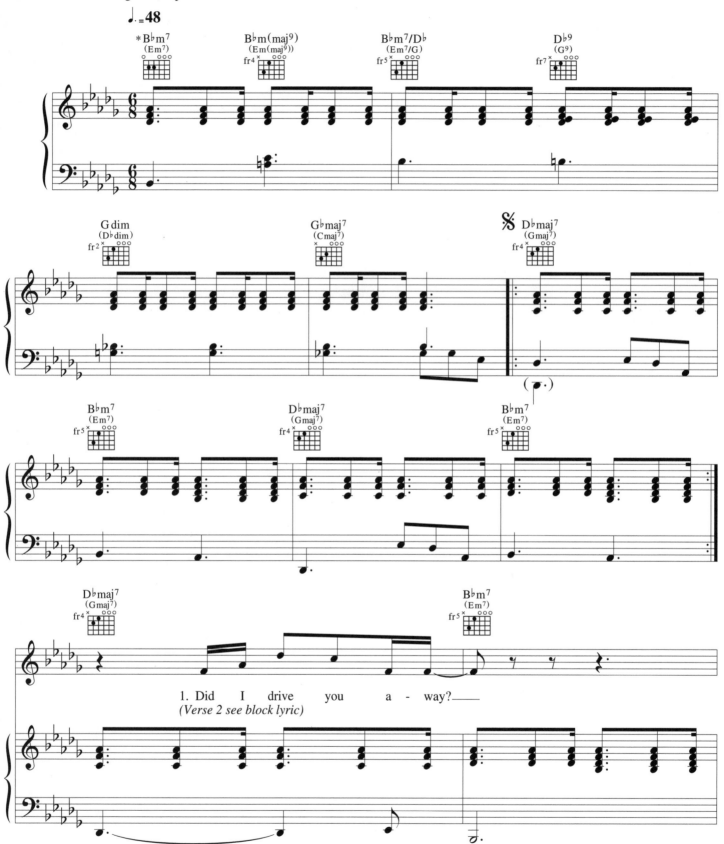

1. Did I drive you a - way?____
(Verse 2 see block lyric)

*Symbols in parentheses represent chord names with respect to capoed guitar (TAB 0 = 6th fret).
Symbols above represent actual sounding chords.

Well I know what you'll say, you'll say____ oh,____

sing one you know.____

But I pro - mise you this,____

I'll al - ways look out for you.

21

Verse 2:
My heart is yours
It's you that I hold on to
That's what I do.
And I know I was wrong
But I won't let you down
Oh, yeah I will, yeah I will
Yes I will.

I said I
I cry I.

YELLOW

Words & Music by Guy Berryman, Jon Buckland, Will Champion & Chris Martin

Guitar Tuned:
① = D♯ ④ = B
② = B   ⑤ = A
③ = G   ⑥ = E

And it was called— yel-low.— So then I took my——

—— turn, oh, what a thing to've— done.——

And it was all— yel-low.—

Your skin,———— oh yeah, your skin and bones——— turn— in - -

Verse 2:
I swam across, I jumped across for you
Oh, what a thing to do
Cos you were all yellow
I drew a line, I drew a line for you
Oh, what a thing to do
And it was all yellow.

Your skin, oh yeah, your skin and bones
Turn into something beautiful
And you know, for you I'd bleed myself dry
For you I'd bleed myself dry.

PARACHUTES

Words & Music by Guy Berryman, Jon Buckland, Will Champion & Chris Martin

HIGH SPEED

Words & Music by Guy Berryman, Jon Buckland, Will Champion & Chris Martin

1. Can a-ny-bo-dy fly___ this thing?___
2. Can a-ny-bo-dy stop___ this thing?___

*Alternate different Gadd9 shapes

Be-fore my head ex - plodes,___ be-fore my head starts___ to ring.

We've been liv - ing life___

in - side a bub-ble.

We've been liv-ing life_____ in - side a bub-ble.

And con - fi - dence in you___ is con - fi - dence in me,

is con - fi - dence in___ high_____ speed.___

1.

2° only (In___ high_____ speed.___)

Instrumental ad lib.

2. G add⁹

High___ speed.___

WE NEVER CHANGE

Words & Music by Guy Berryman, Jon Buckland, Will Champion & Chris Martin

would be ea - sy.

Oh, and I don't have a soul to save.

Yes, and I sin ev - 'ry sin - gle

day.

EVERYTHING'S NOT LOST

Words & Music by Guy Berryman, Jon Buckland, Will Champion & Chris Martin

hop - ing ev - 'ry - thing's not lost.

Verse 2:
When you thought that it was over
You could feel it all around
When everybody's out to get you
Don't you let it drag you down.

So if you even feel neglected *etc.*

LIFE IS FOR LIVING

Words & Music by Guy Berryman, Jon Buckland, Will Champion & Chris Martin

Guitar tuned:

① = D ④ = D
② = B ⑤ = A
③ = G ⑥ = E

if I____ was wrong____ then I'm sor - ry,_____ then

don't let it stand____ in our____ way.____ 2. Cos

my head just aches when I think of_____ the

things that I should - n't have____ done.____ But

ah.

TROUBLE

Words & Music by Guy Berryman, Jon Buckland, Will Champion & Chris Martin

and thought_ of all___ the stu - pid things_ I'd___ said.

2. Oh no, what's this?
(Verse 3 see block lyric)
A spi - der web_ and I'm caught in the mid - dle.

So I turned to run,_____ and thought_ of all___ the stu - pid things_ I'd__

They spun a web___ for me,___ and they spun a web___ for me,___ and they spun a web___

Verse 3:
Oh no, I see a spider web and it's me in the middle.
So I twist and turn, but here am I in my little bubble.

Singing out ah, I never meant to cause you trouble,
Ah, I never meant to do you wrong.
And ah, well if I ever caused you trouble,
Then oh no, I never meant to do you harm.

1/04 (49933)